I0755907

FINISHING LINE PRESS
www.finishinglinepress.com

Jack Imagines a Different Map

poems by

Kevin Brown

Finishing Line Press
Georgetown, Kentucky

Jack Imagines a Different Map

ISBN 979-8-89990-501-8 First Edition

Publisher: Leah Huete de Maines
Editor: Christen Kincaid
Cover Art: Walter Arnold Photography—The Art of Abandonment
Author Photo: Courtney D. Brown
Cover Design: Elizabeth Maines McCleavy

Order online: www.finishinglinepress.com
also available on amazon.com

Author inquiries and mail orders:
Finishing Line Press
PO Box 1626
Georgetown, Kentucky 40324
USA

Contents

"In the middle of life, death comes
to take your measurements. The visit
is forgotten and life goes on. But the suit
is being sewn on the sly."

—from "Black Postcards" by Tomas Tranströmer

Jack Lives Longer Than He Thought

Even before I turned twenty, I believed
I was destined to die
by thirty; my body would betray

me, break down
early, though I found no genetic
flaw in my family nor was I attracted to

accidents. I simply knew.
Three months before thirty,
I was almost

correct, almost found
my fate following delinquent
teenagers on Eisenhower Boulevard,

a dump truck drifting through the
air between us—those proverbial inches—
crushed the car in the left
lane, as if in the midst of a movie

trailer tornado, some angry
Oz clearing off his car
lot, not worried what the debris
might destroy. Even as I survived

thirty, now forty, I know
what my body is bent towards
becoming, as all of ours are, the thought
of which stays with me like spilt milk

in the back seat of that car, spoiled, clinging
to the carpet that cannot come
clean, the smell always in the back
of my mind.

Jack Talks Trade-In

My ball-joints have begun to break.
Engine whines at every stop
sign. My college car finally fading.

The door I once opened for Melissa,
then Julie, jams when I go to load
groceries. Any new car is an upgrade;

they've all gone global
positioning, telling me where
I am and where I am not

and where I could be. The interior smells
like a stereotype, like my father's first
Ford, the only new car he could afford,
bought the year the factory
felt he was foreman

material, could move men
as well as parts to be put together
down the line.

Everything here looks new,
though I know the sheen
will wither, the shellac of wax
will wane or chip before I leave

the lot, a woman's voice repeating,
Recalculating.
Recalculating.
Recalculating.

Jack Makes a Move

In the record store, I pull a used CD from
the rack, Duran Duran's greatest hits,
pretend to read the playlist while watching
a young woman straighten flyers for the latest
local concert as bass beats rattle my spine
like a bottle of pills, smells of perfume
and caramel corn drift in from the hallway.
She wears a college ID in a lanyard between

her breasts, a faded logo on her shirt, a band
that blew my mind in the eighties. She sees me
watching her, so I smile, move to checkout,
tell her of the concert where I bought the band's
last cassette, saw Michael Hutchene seven days before
his suicide. She half hears, tells me, while talking
to her phone, she has not heard of *Inks*, saw the shirt
at Goodwill, knew how good it would look on her.

Jack's Every Day Life

Coffee comes on automatically, 5:48 a.m.
every day, even Saturdays when most sleep in,
a cup and a half to make it through the day.
Gym doors open at 6:30, up the walk

every day, even Saturday, when most sleep in;
workers check clocks if I miss by a minute,
as the gym doors open at 6:30, then walk
to work, past the same secretary for twenty years,

co-workers check clocks if I miss by a minute
while they push papers, one person to another,
pass them to the same secretary for twenty years,
muddle through meetings, pie-shaped prophecies

on papers I push from one person to another
around a leisurely lunch at the desk, side of spreadsheets,
muddle through mundane pie-shaped prophecies.
End one day with a deluxe frozen dinner, or take out,

a leisurely dinner at home, side of spreadsheets,
an early evening, legs across an empty king bed,
End another with take out, or a deluxe frozen dinner,
program the coffee, comes on automatically, 5:48 a.m.

Jack Considers Changing His Life

Eighties anthems echo around
the conversation in Burt's Bar—Joan Jett
loving rock n'roll, another one biting

the dust—a few ballads between for variety,
the same songs we heard at fifteen with fake
IDs, noiseless basketball

on the television behind the bar.
Doug, Mike, and Bill talk of basketball,
the game they play every Wednesday,

the one I once went to every week,
though they know my knees ached since eighteen, know
age takes from us all. Still, they talk of steals

and shots they blocked and didn't. *I want a will,*
I interjected, *thinking about long-term*
life insurance, as well. They paused, looked

at me like I was their parents, in this place,
on a Friday night. Bill bothered
his beer. I told them this would be my last

late night, need to be in bed
by eleven. Mike stopped smiling, stopped
me when I went to leave,

said, *You're barely past forty, not*
dead yet, ordered me a Jack and Coke.
Doug made it a double. I drank it dry,

ordered the next round, said I would see
them later, next week, maybe.

Jack Has Not Outgrown Everything

The night I turned ten, I felt the weight
of a life with double digits, despite
being surrounded by *Star Wars* sheets,
a lightsaber on the table beside
me. Perhaps it was because I learned
that even Darth Vader could die. Perhaps
it was because my friends spoke of funerals,

where sisters who had punched them, pulled their hair,
would cry over their coffins, and cousins
who had left them out of their games of hide
and seek or ghosts in the graveyard would now
regret every moment of fun they had
ever had. I thought such feelings were like
the puberty teenagers talked about,

something to be passed through, gotten over
by the time I turned sixteen. When I turned
ten, I was told to let my imaginary friends
fade away, but Timmy and Tommy grew up
with me, have jobs working the graveyard
shift, spend weekends on my couch, watch
basketball, always cheer for the underdog.

Jack Studies Genealogy and Genetics

My aunt Helen did not die
until she had turned one hundred
and nine. All my aunts
and uncles saw eighty-
five, while my parents passed

sixty, then seventy,
still going. If genetics gives any
hope, I have half a life
left to live, more than forty
more years to find out why

forty more years might
matter, plenty to pass
the time. But I have a hole in my
heart, hypothetically,

my gene perhaps the mutation
proving the rule. Doctors and
stockbrokers warn past
performance is no guarantee

of future success. Every day, buses run
into cars that have careened into
intersections—distracted drivers
calculating how many

years they had left to live—separating
driver from DNA, leaving only
a crumpled car on the side
of the road, a caved-in chromosome.

Doug Considers the Future of Baseball

Doug wants to be frozen—
cryonics, not cryogenics,
he insists—but only his head;
by the time technology
can bring him back, they can build
a better body, one without forty-year
flab and ankles that ache.

Bill sneers, says it sounds too
Six-Million-Dollar-Man-like
for him, talks of Ted Williams,
whose head was supposedly used
as a soccer ball; Mike asks

if a baseball would have been
better. Doug focuses on Williams'
future, how his rebuilt body
and eyes could still see every seam,

see the stitch of every pitch,
hit four hundred for as long
as we all lived. We want a world
of Saturday and Sunday afternoons

sitting on comfortable couches
watching a baseball player
from before we were born
hammer one hit after another, not even
our can of beer breaking a sweat.

Jack Still Has Superstitions

Like the pitcher he once was, leaping
lines—chalk charting the path to first
base, from third base—on his way to and from
the dugout, when he goes back
home, he drives past the park

where his parents picked him up, dropped
him off every spring and summer
day for a decade, passes previous
girlfriends' houses, wonders why he let them

leave—or he left them—wonders where
or who they are now, the same
routine to delay telling his parents
about another promotion

that passed him, another long list
of layoffs he might be on. He remembers
how it felt to hold the ball,
his fingers following the seams to

form a fastball that once fanned fourteen,
remembers what it was like
when he was the one throwing strikes, not
hearing the muffled pop of the mitt

behind him, wondering what went past
when he wasn't paying attention.

Jack Carries All He Can

Faced with fire, I would forego the photo
albums—polaroids of birthday parties
and family trips to the beach held together

by yellowing tape—leave the quilt my
grandmother made, even financial files
for retirement. Doug and I watch

The Jerk, laugh at the only thing Nevin
needed: an ashtray, then a paddle
game, then a remote control, matches,

but not the dog, definitely not the dog.
We make irrational lists at the end
of our lives, ignore our carrying capacity,

allow infinite trips into our houses
or bodies. I would take the basketball
game against our archrival in my senior

season, my free throws forcing overtime,
my steal saving our high school souls,
or I would pick up my prom, carry it

like a damsel in distress across the threshold
of memory. I did not get drunk or lucky,
but both possibilities were present, teased

as high as my date's hair. I would carry
them both and more if my stiffening body
could bear their weight, if I could find them
in the flames.

Jack's Co-Workers Double Down

A group congregates in Kathy's cubicle
every Monday morning, talks about
what they won (and lost) that weekend
at casinos, the track, even

cricket matches. On Wednesdays,
they wonder what they would do
if they won the lottery
or if they had only one

more day, maybe one more
month, to live, how they would create
lives they would lead: Fridays full

of family and friends, weekends
indistinguishable from what were once
work days, Tuesdays turning over again

and again, bronzing bodies as they
break down. For now, they read
reports, sit at spreadsheets that always
add up, the inevitable march

of math and logic, the dealer
collecting the cards, the house
winning one more hand.

Jack Receives Spam Promising an Enhancement Bonus

I know I've lost a little spring,
left behind the half-step in the half-court,
one of many moves, left it like my high school

yearbook, my freshman year, chosen Most
Likely to Succeed. Paired with the geekiest girl,
the one who worked on physics on the bus,

calculated vectors and force while we
made ice into projectiles, launched them
from open windows, measured the force
of our fun. Her best black dress set off

her braces; my tie, slightly loosened, skinny
as her hips, my jacket, blue as the *Miami*
Vice sky, bright as my condescension.
She wrote beside our picture in handwriting

that looped around our names: *Stay true to yourself*
and you'll go far. But I know no pill
or powder will give me the feeling

that followed a fourteen-point quarter
or when whatever girlfriend I was with giggled
like every other girl I knew, touched my
arm, told me I was too much, just *too* much.

Jack Describes Some Odd Discussions

My tendinitis talks to me more
than it once did—longer conversations
than college chats between
intramural games or huddled

at the half. It asks me what I'm
thinking when I stay out past
midnight on New Year's or play
basketball with boys who barely look

legal for work, discuss their pre-med majors
while we get water. Yet there are times
I can outargue it, can convince my
cartilage to cushion the blows

my body receives, soar past the
nineteen-year-old, the court
like the trampoline the Tidwells owned
when I was eight. But my back

always taps me on itself, tells me
to turn around, look at myself
in the mirror, asks me if I think
I'm fooling anyone besides myself.

Jack Considers Dessert

> "A 10-year study found that overweight
> people had heart attacks 8.2 years earlier
> than normal-weight victims." —*Men's Health*

What would eight more years matter?
What would two thousand nine hundred
ninety-five more days of life lead to
without chocolate or caffeine? Why
would we cease smoking or drinking—
white wine or micro-brews—to gain
more days of game shows and rehearsed
reality, more lives of lawyers
and detectives? What would eight years
of unlimited texts while driving away
from work after 8.2 hours mean?
Why watch one more one-named chef
show us soufflés and tarts, an ultimate
omelet we will never make? What's one
more weekday night spent with a sundae,
one spot already staining the shirt, vanilla
ice cream, caramel corkscrewing to the center
of our souls, chopped peanuts and Oreo
cookies sprinkled over top, generously,
like lost years, with a cherry on the top?

Jack Does Not Play Games, Anymore

We played Office Bingo my first few
years, squares of administrators' actions
and catchphrases—Simmons' six sips

of coffee before presentations, Clark's
Don't-reinvent-the-wheel-laden memos.
In our cubicles, we made membership cards
for the Future Corpses of America.

I served two terms as Vice-President
of Disorganization. No one knows how long
they lasted. A new hire suggested Current
Corpses, was fired after three days.

We needed to pretend work was not
important, that our lives mattered more
than ten-hour days followed by cocktail
chasers, but we were nothing more than
boys and girls playing games like Hi Ho!

Cherry-O or Chutes and Ladders, let
adults tell us what time to wake up,
when to be in bed. We whined

about working weekends when we wanted
to fly kites, a key tied to the tail,
hoped life would strike like lightning.

Jack Talks Statistics

We tell stories about fathers, men who
hit us ground balls, men who now sit
at computers searching for symptoms
they might have one day. We exchange
BMIs and HDLs like ERAs and RBIs,
trade troubles like baseball cards we passed
back and forth on Doug's back porch.

Bill wants to talk about films—Clint Eastwood's
career or Tim Allen's latest—but I mention
a study I saw on TV, complications
of heart bypass, stop everyone eating—egg-
beaters, whole grain toast. Mike sits
silently in the corner, chews buttermilk
pancakes, syrup dripping from his lips,
whipped cream creasing his slight smile.

Jack Can't Shake a Cold

My friend who turned forty
forewarned me about all age
will take away: the name of my
fourth-grade girlfriend, lived
five, maybe six, houses down Elm,
called Patti Pigtails, despite her hair

shorn too short to tie in a ribbon,
despite my knowing no one
named Patti; the ability to see
clearly and closely, my neck
at an awkward angle, technology

turned against me, makes me move
as methodically as my parents.
They did not say what remains:
the cough I caught from a co-worker
two months ago, survived two

doctors, three antibiotics,
a too-tired child who should
have been in bed hours ago,
willfully remaining half-awake;

an achy ankle caused by a mis-
step on a steep staircase, went for
a cup of coffee, not a cut on
a basketball court. Everything
lingers but life, fades faster
than fourth-grade love.

Jack Wants a Mnemonic Device for Life

In seventh grade, I tried Roy G.
Biv—a cornucopia
of colors' names, Crayola crayons

the only way I knew half
the rainbow range—
then moved to planets,

a song about my very educated
mother who just served us nine pizza
pies. Those pizzas are gone now

we've entered a new century,
Pluto put out of our orbit, disappointing
those too-small twelve-year-olds
who believed in an over-achieving

asteroid. I try every trick to remember
meetings and projects, decorate my desk
with the spectrum of post-its, enter dates

and deadlines in my laptop and phone,
even magnet calendars to the fridge,
as if I had obsessive children

whose work I wanted to show off,
as if the sheer number of notes will nudge
my neurons toward memory, spark

my mind to read that report on how
consumers cannot remember what
they really want, though they carry
lists everywhere, lay out their lives.

Jack Remembers Reading (Skimming, Actually) *The Odyssey*

The Cyclops, of course, the story everyone
thinks they know, and the one about the whirlpool
and the cliff, where we get *between a rock*
and a hard place. And the Sirens, always

the Sirens, women who pull us us toward
the rocks of our ruin, who we reinvent
to resemble the women we want, ignore
our destruction. Throughout college, Chris

commented on them, talked too much
about temptation, too much about Melanie,
the woman who wanted him to adjust
his art major, follow her father to his office
every day, begin in business, support her

and his hypothetical children, even wanted
him to abandon his Lotus-eating friends,
so he left her on the shore. He saw her
in his sleep, sheets like mainsails torn
from snapped mizzenmasts. He became

a business major the next semester,
preached practicality, told us
we needed something strong,
some stake that would not break
despite the storm, despite the song.

Jack Goes Back to College

She smiled at me the year I turned twenty,
sitting in Sociology of the Family, marriage
her major, but one more elective for me,

as I wandered from course to course, no course
to direct my decisions. I followed the six-year
plan, Accounting the most practical by then;
she graduated in three and a half, got who

she wanted before her sophomore year. I saw her
again at Homecoming, I, in town to visit
my failing father; she, there to see who she
once was, before Billy and Phil and Scott

and Tony took away her younger years,
before the children, names I forgot before she
showed me their pictures. She had already
seen her dorm, visited her old room—

though they've added air conditioning—
had even walked on the soccer field, only seen
at night before now. She had even seen
Dr. Hall, told him she still remembers the five

characteristics of a successful marriage.
She told me she still needed practice
with number four, and smiled a smile
full of furniture, as I walked away again.

Jack Is Glad He's Not a Surgeon

On my way to work one morning, I noticed
a billboard of bodies, skin flayed away,
leaving only men with muscles, some

macabre—or medical—museum exhibit.
And I was reminded of Ralph, the cat
I kept for one semester of sophomore

biology, whose muscles I memorized,
made mine, not by bending over a book,
but by modeling at the mirror, moving

my arm one way, flexing my fingers
another, trying to see how I connected
and how I did not. But then we cut

that cat open, found intestines that looked
like mangled macaroni and cheese
(at least to two teenagers). *Dead from*

disease, Ms. Campbell commented,
Cancer, probably, leaving us to study
suffering's causes and its effects. I

wonder what that fifteen-year-old might
find if he could map my muscles now,
could cut me open—scalpel scraping

sternum on the way down: lungs
atrophied from inactivity, the empty
space from when I gave my gall

bladder away before thirty, and my
heart, unscarred, but barely beating.

Jack Reminisces With an Old Friend

Those who are twenty years
younger tell me I'm being left
behind, try to turn me on to their
technology—would label me a Luddite,

if they knew what one was—their
iPhones and Blackberries buzzing with breaking
business, while I wait for my email
to load; they Skype with clients I can't find

in the phone book. But I remember
what I was told two decades ago
by a young man from the mail
room—no hot shot Harvard grad—
who would walk with me

to lunch, even after he passed
over me with his first promotion
on his path to company president,
told me what Willy Loman was told

was wrong, that who you know
must matter. He tells me even still, every
Wednesday when we meet for drinks,
the only forty-five minutes

his phone is silent; we talk about the lives
we once lived, enjoy the only time
I don't need to wonder
what kind of whiskey he wants.

Jack Hears Some Helpful Financial Advice

Walking to Wednesday
drinks, she stopped us—
a young woman wearing hemp
shorts and Chacos, a smile

reminding me she was not working
in the middle of the week—
asked us to give to a good cause.
Though no longer a young man
from the mail room, he felt the need
to explain his reluctance:

But I had a recent retirement rollover, you see; I'll grant the goodness of the cause, do not disagree, but my money must move, not play dead like a dog, need new tricks to keep up. And gas has gone up again; a fill-up for my Ford Ranger costs as much as my monthly payment, or almost. Of course, I want a cure for cancer, a means to a medicine to ameliorate MS symptoms or whatever it was you said, but now is not the time to tap my resources.

Walking away, he found
a five in his pocket,
produced it with the joy

Jonas Salk must have felt,
backtracked, handed
it to her humbly.

Doug's Self-Diagnoses

I'm going to die, Doug tells us at dinner,
news we meet with tinks of toasts, sounds
of celebration, same as the week before,
the one before that. *No, I'm serious,*

but our talk has moved to teams who could
push to the playoffs. Doug develops
every ailment, from Albers-Schönberg
disease to Zygomycosis, prompting him

to call one of the medical facilities
or practitioners he has programmed
into his phone, from oncologists
to proctologists, even, *just in case,*

his gynecologist. He claims a wisdom
we lack, says he will be prepared
when a doctor diagnoses him with cancer
or curare poisoning, as if his fate

is unlike ours, as if we cannot carry
the weight he believes he was born
with, set it on the restaurant table in front
of us, walk away without the leftovers.

Jack is Cornered at a Convenience Store by an Old Man Who Wants to Tell Someone Everything That's Wrong with the World

and people move like maniacs today, honking horns and riding my bumper, but not just in cars that whip and zip, feel like I'm standing still at sixty, but even when they walk past me on their way to work, earphones and iPods, walking by trees and flowers and people, for god's sake, they don't even see, like my students who sit sullenly in the backs of classrooms, ballcaps keeping me from seeing eyes wander, try to hide their texting under their desks, as if I think they're looking at their privates, just like their long-sleeved shirts, hide tattoos, tell which gang grabbed them in middle school, and the guy up front here, covers his Koran before we check out as if we don't know what he's up to, Al-Jazeera playing on the radio, I read the newspapers, know which way the world is headed, I mean, have you seen the way kids dress today, pants around their knees, that says it all, yes sir, that says it all

Jack Hears What We Can and Cannot Carry

When Wendy went to bury
Bill, she wanted a graveside service—
though he would have complained
about the cost—wanted
her daughter and son to see

the cemetery, see where their father's body was
buried. As we tossed dirt
on the casket—an underhanded throw
no different than the one we used when we greeted

the groom and bride
with birdseed not a decade before—
Wendy turned toward us, talked
of how her boy believed Bill

was god, had worshiped him, wanted
to be him, wondered who he would be
now; how Bill's bad behavior could not
be redeemed, how he had demanded his daughter kiss
him when he smelled of piss

and despair, worried whether that girl's grudge
could find a grave; but most of all she spoke of love
now lost, the lives of love
they could not now live, lost to the grave
and the ground. Mike shook

his head from side to side, wiped away
Wendy's words, muttered to himself,
mumbled *no* before he said it simply
but clearly: No. He turned Wendy toward

the half-filled hole, *It won't fit.*
You have to let it live on here
with us. The coffin cannot hold it all.

Jack Unwillingly Attends a Retirement Dinner

He turns from the stage, and I expect
an amusing anecdote, some story about
practical jokes he and the retiree played

together, locked their manager in the women's
bathroom at a conference, perhaps,
or some gossip from my first week,

how my tie was as tacky as the cheap
chicken they always serve at such dinners.
He tells me grief is the hardest thing

in his life, that, since his wife went away—
woman cancer, he calls it—he wakes
every day, even Saturdays and Sundays,

at seven, knows he has nothing until nine
at night when he will turn out the light,
wait to wake again. He cannot look

at the calendar's cavernous days and weeks,
what's left of his lonely life. He comes
closer, whispers, *I didn't even like him;*

I wanted to kill three hours, looks at
his watch wearily, waits for the speech
that has not started to finally be finished.

Jack Negotiates

I have given away a lifetime of lives
already, traded ten years in a teenage
auto accident, wanted to see my parents
retire outside a condo in Panama

City and tell embarrassing stories
about my brother and sister and me.
And when my gall bladder gave out
in my early thirties—thought someone

had found a way to adjust my aorta
with a crescent wrench—I told death
to take twenty, even thirty years,
just for five more, maybe ten. I have

changed my approach, now send diplomats
like a dad in a divorce does lawyers,
thinking only, *Not the children. Please,*
not the children, anymore.

Jack Discusses Children

At lunch with four co-workers, all
married, not to each other, not all
of them their first (even second
for Sam), ten children between
them—four, three, two, one—then
me, the one who will die alone,
they say, nothing but a thin sheet and
a stranger to take me to the other

side, my name unknown once I'm gone,
carved in a stone in lot 4B, the corner
of the cemetery no one visits. I nod
my head gravely, wait for the quesadillas
before responding, tell them renown seems
a poor reason for reproduction, that two
generations from now, their great-grandchildren

will not know they were, that leaving loved
ones who hold our hands is still leaving;
they stay here while we go somewhere (or
nowhere) alone. I have killed the conversation
and can already see next week: burritos
from a box I reheat in the employee lounge,
the microwave smelling of burnt popcorn.

Moonwalk

After twenty years, we peer through
the window of our chemistry
class, where Doug dozed

daily, drooled on his desk
like his dog, the mutt
Mike hit on the highway
the following year—it lived,
limped the next eleven

years. We don't linger long
at the room where Ms. Gray taught
English, the mural of *Moby-Dick*
on the back wall still looming over
juniors, Ishmael, still lost at sea,
as we were when we could not pretend poetry

mattered; even onomatopoeia
could not make us chuckle,
though we laid down lines

of our own for bands
that broke up as often as Jacquie and Chad,
who somehow managed to marry

each other anyway. The buffet
in the gym—local barbecue
with the smell of molasses
balanced by the tang

of age—does not remind us
of dances we ditched or basketball
games gone into overtime,
the conversation now chit-chat
about children and wives and the cost

of it all, though I want to walk the halls
one last time, wearing a Walkman
playing "Thriller," move
like Michael Jackson once did.

Jack Wonders What Happened to CompuServe

Twenty-five years ago, Mrs. Kitzmiller
taught me typing, used her ruler
to rap my knuckles when my focus fell

to the keys of a rusted Royal
or Underwood. She tapped out time
with it: *a-s-d-f-space-j-k-l-semi-space.*
Now, my boss uses the Blackberry

the company bought for his five-year
anniversary to tell me,
again, to begin a blog

to sell our services, push our product, no more
long letters telling potential clients
what I CAN DO for them, email
an inconvenience for those who never played

Pong. I hear twenty-somethings twitting
or tweeting to one another
or clients they collect

like friends or followers, the clicks
of their keypads footsteps that follow me
to my office, their phone's vibrations
a shudder I feel stealing over my old soul.

Jack Considers Options He No Longer Has

My parents kept worksheets from sixth
grade. I wanted to be a surgeon, explored
encyclopedias they bought for my brother

and sister, saw opaque pages of muscles,
digestive and circulatory systems laid over
a skeleton to become the body I would

become. I wanted to heal hurting hearts,
see what they felt like surrounded by my fingers.
Looking up *aorta*, I found *astronaut*—

a picture of a space capsule entering earth's
atmosphere, a fiery angel with a message
of the life I could live. I moved to math

in middle school, then to teaching in high school,
wanted to make myself the man who stood
before me twice a day, who showed me sines

and cosines could matter more than
mere numbers, tied tangents into a circle
surrounding us all. My parents shipped

the encyclopedias—long out of date—
to the Salvation Army, the heart buried
beneath pages and pages of outer space.

Jack's Uncle Lives Life Without a Word of Complaint

As kids, my cousin and I would wonder
which was worse: going blind or deaf.

We were shallow, said we would miss
beauty—neighborhood girls whose breasts

were just becoming or guitar solos by Steve
Vai or Eddie Van Halen—but we knew not

to hope it happened. We never wondered,
though, what it would be like to be made

mute, what words we would miss most, not until
twenty-five years later when his father can not

speak—throat cancer, they thought, though
he had never smoked. We watch him loll

in his La-Z-Boy, unable to cheer his Dolphins
when they score—*not often*, he used to say.

We walk with him in the mall; he wishes he
could whistle at the way a woman sways,

regrets the one word he did not say often
enough, the one his generation did not

speak of, tries to tell us with his eyes,
his tongue and lips useless, saying nothing.

Jack Remembers Almost Everything

In middle school, I focused on
the future: the day I would drive
my date to dinner

at DePalma's, the day every May
I would get out of school
for the summer, the day one May

I would get out for good.
Doug now describes me as
his definition of old—*When the past*

is more present than the future—
as I have little to look forward to:
aches from my ancestors, visit
too often; a rapidly receding

retirement where I'll spend my
money to pay a stranger to strip
me every week for a bath; a fifty-five
hour work week, monotony broken only by beers

in a bar we found at fifteen.
So I spend evenings finding friends
from high school

on Facebook, send messages about the highlights
of Homecoming, our yearly run-in
with our rivals, or yearn for yearbook

beauties—Michelle or Melanie,
maybe Jacqui. Yet when I work
from home, I forget the file

for the mid-week meeting, leave it
in my office cabinet, somewhere between
graduation and *growing up.*

What Jack Refuses to Focus On

His father's fall as he went to the mailbox
one morning; shelves of Lean Cuisine spaghetti,
lasagna, French bread pizza, chicken with sugar
snap peas, devil's food cake, banana pudding,
cherries jubilee; reports he did not run
on Friday afternoon; a new location for Lowe's,
built on land where his elementary school
spread out for sixty-two years before
the bigger one on highway 64; the water
stain on the ceiling tile, resembles Florida,
perhaps Maryland; his spin move to the basket
that still works, most of the time, the way
his back does not; the doctor's appointment
his HMO makes for him, as if his mother
still scheduled his life; plaid slippers his father
wore to pick up the paper every morning,
the right one always slightly in front of the left,
eager to see what happened overnight; the twenty-
four-year-old in the office next to his;
computers that can do taxes while playing
chess and carrying on a conversation;
the barking cough that couldn't be
cancer; the forty-six-year-old police
officer who had a heart attack while walking
his dog—reporters said what they always say:
completely unexpected, unpredictable,
no one saw this coming, had just been to
the doctor; the CPA exam he failed
six times; Hackney Distribution's account
he has been unable to balance for two
months, stares at columns so long they slide
from side to side like his childhood television
when the vertical hold went out; finding
his mother's hearing aids in the kitchen
trash, just beneath a banana she only ate
half of; the scar on Ryan's skull; the metallic
ping knocking on the underside of his hood.

Chris Explains a Life Well-Lived

Not by not staying, by boarding a
bus for New York to ask and
ask and ask for acting jobs or
sequestering myself, finishing the
screenplay I've scribbled on letter-
head through months of meetings
that have moved me to apathy.

But by dying after decades of the
same sandwich—turkey and Swiss
on rye, light on the mayo—as the
same break between the same work
that helped support the same woman
and children, the same life so many
believe is soulless, bereft of courage.

Jack Watches a Co-Worker Keep It Together

We're all professionals here: men wear
collars stiff with starch; women wear suits
more often than men; others staple or collate
copies of our presentations; we don't need
to know such capabilities. So when
the twenty-two-year-old intern saves seats

for a row of friends, makes the Wednesday
meeting into a high school assembly, leaves
Jeff standing; or a budget committee officer
changes his incompetence into Jeff's, shifts
blame as smoothly as his leased Lexus slides
from second to third; or a nameless middle
manager stands too close when questioning

his company commitment, his hand clinches
once, only once, as if trying to hold on to
that one second his sophomore year when he
buried a bully with one punch, when everyone
believed he was better than he was, that one
moment more than twenty years ago now,
long since slipped from his fist.

Jack is Quick, Narrowly Avoids Death

I was almost hit by a hearse
this morning; it moved so fast,
must have believed

a funeral is a fire,
the body in the back the one way
to extinguish it, leave people relieved,

not grieved. If this were a scene in a movie,
a matinee my friends and I wanted to try
ten dollars on, we would leave with shaken

heads, so heavy-handed
we would demand our
disbelief back, talk about it over tacos, canned

caliente the soundtrack, a starter of
queso fundido so spicy it makes
the movie seem subtle—*Okay, I get*
it, he looks both ways, but death runs

him over regardless; Mike mutters,
It comes around the corner too
quickly, can't predict

or expect it, catches him
unaware—before moving to more
important matters: mortgages

barely made; Bixby's unsurprising
unemployment; the looming
layoff of the NBA, the legality

of its lockout, and what we will watch
instead. We leave in different
directions to collect our cars, stand
on separate street corners, wait one

second longer,
then two,

before stepping into the street.

Jack's Co-Worker in the Corner Cubicle Brought Her Worries to Work

Her headaches kept coming,
returned regularly, every morning
for a month, then stopped. She thought

they might be migraines,
did not know what caused them,
thought there could be a tumor,
or, even worse, an aneurysm.

She did not know what one
was, what one felt like, or what
one did other than dictate death,
but she did know she did not want

to find out, avoided doctors or
Wikipedia. She wore simple
clothing, modest, at all times,

and did not take showers
when the headaches hit
in case she collapsed. She imagined

how her hands and arms would be
angled, which way her feet would
splay, whether a bit of blood

would trickle from her nose, darken
enough to reflect the radio's reporting
on someone's sudden death
somewhere else.

One a Day

I heard the radio repeat a story
from television: septuagenarians
on Suzukis, Hondas,
and, of course, Harleys, protesting

some Senate bill about health
care I had never heard of.
A co-worker told me of a fad

diet: six miles of walking,
with water—fourteen glasses—
every day, not only to keep the weight

away, but lengthen one's life
by a decade. In the left lane,
a grandmother gunned her motorcycle,
a patch on the back of her jean

jacket: *Get busy living, or get busy dying.*
She sat on saddlebags: seven, maybe
eight, containers of pills, enough
bottles of water to help a family
of four survive the rest of their long lives.

The Exception That Proves the Rule

I wondered when the pain would appear
this morning and where—my back from last
week, left knee from the month before, or

somewhere new, my injuries moving as often
as I did in college, no apartment or townhouse
gave me the life I wanted, but the aches

never arrived. Walking to work, a woman
I watched saw me move, slowed, smiled
as if I might matter for more than just that

moment, as if I were the boat she were about
to board, a cruise she had waited to take since she
was fourteen. And when the early afternoon let-down

of life did not come, I did not need to dream
of fourteen, twenty-four, even thirty-four;
instead, I ended the day with a simple spaghetti

supper, the balance of basil and oregano,
a gasp of garlic behind every bite.

Jack Listens to the Language People Use

When Wendy told us she had lost her
husband, we wondered at her word
choice: *lost*, as if Bill had become
a boy, become an eight-year-old
lost in a grocery store as the PA

system echoed his name through
aisles crammed with consumers and
comestibles, everything but Bill.
But what word should she use,
after having heard hospital hedging

for five months? Bill began with
anomalies and insufficiencies, progressed
to pseudo-police speak as his heart
was arrested, as if it will be arraigned,
kept away from law-abiding body

parts for some time. Everything
became acute or chronic, and it ended
in failure, as it always does, as if
we are surprised again and again by our
bodies' breaking down, as if death is

not in our design. And when we ask
Wendy how she is, we do not want
to hear how she is falling to pieces
or falling apart (*like a cheap suit,*
my friend Mark often adds); no,

we want to know how she is holding
up or holding it together—whatever
it is—want to believe that Bill
behaved like a boy, became
distracted in a grocery store, spent

too long looking at comic books while
waiting on Wendy, a story we will
laugh about at a cookout at their house
several years from now, gathered
to celebrate one more of Bill's birthdays.

Jack Overhears Misguided Men and Women, Who are Well-Intentioned

And what would I expect to hear
at a friend's funeral, if not rude
platitudes people pass along to deny

death its power? People tell his wife
Wendy that she will see him soon
enough, that he is in a better place

beyond, that he is not contained in
the coffin, that is *just* a shell. But
we did not watch a soul score

forty-four points in our high school
championship, did not witness a wisp
walk a newly-wedded Wendy out

the church, did not speed to a spirit's
bedside when she called, watch
it seep through the ceiling. No,

the body is Bill or Bill became
the body, and no clichés can keep him
away from the grave, whatever is left
of him gone to where language goes to die.

Jack Remembers Where He Came From

I come from a mining man—
my grandfather—moved
coal with only a shovel

and sweat until dust leeched
the life from his lungs. I never
knew him, met him

before my memories
began, must imagine what he
might think of me, whether what I do
is work—managing imaginary

manufacturing, shifting unseen
items from one warehouse
to another, shoveling numbers
from this spreadsheet to that,

back the next day. Only sweat
when I meet with managers,
describe what I do every day, why
it might matter to me or anyone

else. Those meetings or something
I cannot see—the dust of despair,
perhaps—will leech the life out of me.

Jack Reads the Future

Of course, I saw white-haired
grandparents, my own and others'
cushioned in a pillow-top

casket, stooped bodies bent back
to a more natural-looking state,
lips always too red,
as if death wore lipstick.

I knew older people passed on—
as we say in the South, polite
even in death—heard of teenage

tragedies, those who drove their
own demise, graduation tassels
found in floorboards, either too much

alcohol or too much fun, lives
lived too loud for the body.
It was not until I saw Ryan's

twenty-two-year-old skull
shaved for surgery and sewn
back together, his scars spelling

my name, that I knew his fate
would be mine as time turns
on us all, turns us all into

memories on a mantle, only seen
when the blinds on the bay
window are closed, removing the glare.

Jack Feels Cursed

When I am sixty or seventy, maybe
more, if I am lucky enough to live
so long, the doctor will walk in to where
I have been sitting, shivering

for twenty minutes, maybe
thirty, mostly naked, in the side
chair if the nurse cares

about my comfort, otherwise, legs dangling
from the butcher-papered
table, set up for a second

grader to color, pathogens
perhaps or viruses that have visited
me over the years, though not what I will
be there to hear. The scene is similar
to twenty-two-year-old Ryan's
when he heard his brain

was broken, that drains and drugs
would not work, allow him
to die at twenty-nine. Or for Diane, traded
a breast to save her
heart, now watches warily, waiting
to be betrayed by a lump or bump

in the night that will send
her back to the knife-wielding man, a B-movie heroine
fated to return to

the house where he hides.
When my turn comes, though, I will not hear him
say *cancer* or *positive*; I will only hear
what I feel like saying: *fuck*.

He will tell me that the fucker has spread
to my major organs, that fucko will only force
me to fade faster, that fuckery

will simply sap my strength, cut my life
shorter than it will be. I will not hear him

say how sorry he is, and no scientific
syntax or Latinate lingo will lessen
the force of the Germanic
diagnosis behind everything

he says: *You're fucked.*

Jack is Rudely Awakened

The four a.m. phone call comes
like a heart attack; my heart stops,
starts again. But I have not died,
nor has anyone I know,

as far as I know, a motel's
malfunctioning phone, same
as the sink stopper with a slow leak,
a morning shave made more difficult.

No one knows the number
to tell me if death has come
as it does, like a four a.m. phone call
or like the long letters my seventh-grade

girlfriend used to write in the summers,
described every detail—the taste
and appearance of her paste-like
oatmeal or soggy, sugar-laden

cereal, the milk blue or brown,
or the kiss she gave a stuffed bear
named Bonzo, her fuzz-laden lips
only stopped moving when asleep.

I knew the endings of those letters
before the beginning, knew before
I turned the twelfth or thirteenth

perfectly perforated page, the closing:
With love, if I was lucky;
otherwise, *Sincerely*.

Jack Decides Against Becoming Immortal

The cubicle congregation had gathered
on Tuesday morning, Lisa looking
at her screen, she the one who noticed
the news: *Some science guy says we would live*

to be one thousand years old.
Even middle managers stopped,
only on the outskirts

pretended to mull
over a meeting they would make
us attend. *Hasn't he seen vampire movies,*
not that tween Twilight

crap, but real ones,
where the vampire hates his fate?
though Lisa looks like she would trade
all her tomorrows for a paradise

of pudding pops and people
who wouldn't judge her love of them.

The scientist says we would be pain free,
but he only measures the material,
not the nine hundred more years
of the tedium of traffic

jams and long lines behind
coupon counters, the nine hundred more years
of divorce and disorienting death—
they can't cure car crashes, can they?—
or nine hundred more years of reading

reports like the ones on my desk,
measure everything
but what matters. Perhaps vampires
view a long life

differently because their mouths have met
our marrow, tasted our life
blood, seen our emptiness
before biting into the nothingness
of our necks.

Persistence

When the winds came—storm of the century,
newscasters said—they tore four trees from
their trunks, broke them like bones—the tibia,
perhaps, or a collarbone an eighth grader
had to have set by surgery after a football
injury—jagged against the newly blue sky.
The absence left unlevel ground, bits of
sawdust and bark, a bald spot in an aging
backyard. Grass is growing again where it
once was, on the edges for now, but leaving
no doubt where it is heading.

Ants have invaded the house, the dishwasher
the perfect plan of entrance. Not like an army—
too easily killed or removed, at least redirected—
but like consumers after Christmas, queuing
to complain about unwrapped and unwanted
presents, seeking minor, yet sweet satisfaction.
They tell others instead of simply savoring it
themselves. Winter will come, and we will forget
the annoyance of ants and grass as they die,
but in March, maybe April, even May,
if we look for them, we will find them beneath
our boots and dishes, insistently living for
the day or month they were made for.

Jack Imagines a Different Map

Lisa talked about life expectancy,
a report she read online that morning,
how a man who moves from Mississippi
to Maine might move the date of his
death back a decade. I wondered

where I might fall in such averages,
knew that my having a heart attack
next week would need to be balanced
by a man in Minnesota who managed

one hundred and ten, or perhaps I
would be the wizened one, countered
by the early death of someone my age,
a forty-year-old father who leaves his
wife with three children: Chad and Sam,
the twins; Melissa, their baby girl.

And I wondered if there were a place
I might move where a tumor does not
take Ryan before he turns thirty, a state
or city where statistics no longer exist,
where charts and graphs don't belong,
and life lasts as long as we can stand it.

Jack Sees Clearly in the Dark

My friends took me to the Lost Sea—
a local attraction most locals only enter
in elementary school. We heard about
caves and crags carved out, though
I still never know the difference

between stalagmites and stalactites.
The guide turned out the lights,
surrounded us with a darkness deep as

despair. Though we could not see
our selves, hands moved back
and forth in front of faces; one
young woman whispered, *This feels like*
death. Darkness is as much like death

as walking underwater is like being lame.
We could still hear our heartbeats, think
about what we might make for dinner,
consider our ancestors who existed here
or those who died elsewhere, like my Uncle

Louis, lost at sea in the second world war,
those who made the same mistakes we will,
misunderstood death. I stood looking
into the darkness, tried to find the reflectors
they placed on rocks to guide us to this spot.

Acknowledgments

Thanks to the following journals for publishing some of these poems in earlier incarnations: *Red Earth Review; Soundings Review; drafthorse; Technoculture; Natural Bridge; Caduceus; Concho River Review; Ibbetson Street; Slipstream; Map Literary; The Milo Review; Pudding Magazine; Rappahannock Review; SLAB Literary Magazine; Hawai'i Pacific Review; Third Wednesday; Spry; Pilgrimage; All Roads Will Lead You Home; Agave.*

Thanks to my peers and professors at Murray State University for the feedback and support you gave me when I was working on my degree and these poems.

Thanks to my students over the years whose work and conversations and friendships have not only made me a better writer, but a better teacher.

Thanks to my colleagues at Lee University, where I was a professor when I wrote these poems, for their encouragment as both a writer and a teacher.

Thanks to my friends and family who continue to celebrate my successes in writing.

Thanks to Courtney, who truly celebrates successes in writing and every other aspect of life. Her joy helps me keep from viewing the world as Jack often does in these pages.

Kevin Brown is a high school English teacher in Nashville, TN. He has published three previous books of poetry: *Liturgical Calendar: Poems* (Wipf and Stock); *A Lexicon of Lost Words* (winner of the Violet Reed Haas Prize for Poetry, Snake Nation Press); and *Exit Lines* (Plain View Press). He also has a memoir, *Another Way: Finding Faith, Then Finding It Again,* and a book of scholarship, *They Love to Tell the Stories: Five Contemporary Novelists Take on the Gospels.* You can find out more about him and his work on social media sites at @kevinbrownwrites or at http://kevinbrownwrites.weebly.com/.

www.ingramcontent.com/pod-product-compliance
Lightning Source LLC
LaVergne TN
LVHW090537110826
845146LV00003B/1137

* 9 7 9 8 8 9 9 9 0 5 0 1 8 *